Witness

Witness

A. BELIEVER

CITI OF
BOOKS

CITIOFBOOKS, INC.
3736 Eubank NE Suite A1
Albuquerque, NM 87111-3579
www.citiofbooks.com
Hotline: 1 (877) 389-2759
Fax: 1 (505) 930-7244

Ordering Information:

Quantity sales. Special discounts are available on quantity purchases by corporations, associations, and others. For details, contact the publisher at the address above.

Printed in the United States of America.

ISBN-13:   Softcover   978-1-960952-62-2
                  eBook   978-1-960952-63-9

Library of Congress Control Number: 2023907601

Foreword

In 2013, I wrote and published through a vanity press, a book I had titled "You Have Got to Be Kidding".

The book chronicled my life from late June 1961 to August 2020 and was based on what I believed had been a remarkable series of instances of amazing good luck. After my wife of 57 years passed away, I decided to read the Bible, and I did so. It took about six months to read from Genesis to Revelation and when I was finished, I wasn't quite sure of what I had read. I knew the words but was unable to make a coherent understanding of what I had read. It was then that my daughter led me to a series of Bible lessons on the Internet from a program titled "The Shepherd's Chapel". Ministered by a father and son who were pastors, they presented hour-long programs that taught the meaning of the Bible chapter by chapter and verse by verse.

Then I discovered that they also presented a reading list of each book where you could select a book and go through it from beginning to end, chapter by chapter, verse by verse. I began with the Book of Genesis and am currently in Ecclesiastes. I had what one might call a "revelation" about a year or so ago as I was watching one of the episodes. After living for 79 years and having a passing knowledge of the Bible and not being a regular church attendee, I had experienced periods when I attended a church regularly for a time, then stopped attending for various reasons. I believed in God, but never really gave that much thought, my belief was superficial at best, although I did try and live by what I understood of the Ten Commandments.

From this point on, I will chronicle those events I initially attributed to "luck". I will let you decide if they were just that, or if there was a much more powerful force at work.

One day, watching an episode of The Chapel, I was jolted by the realization that all those instances that I had written of in the book were not due to luck but were, in fact, instances of "Divine Intervention". I realized that all the things I was referring to could not, in all probability, be attributed to "luck". That would be statistically improbable. Additionally, the magnitude of many of the cases was such that luck wouldn't explain it. As an example, in 1986 I had a myocardial infarction at the age of 44. I was flown to Duke where I underwent a five-vessel bypass procedure. When I woke up from the surgery, the doctors told me that because of all the running I had done while on active duty in the Marine Corps, my heart had created numerous bypasses around blockages. Why is this not just "luck"?

I will attempt to illustrate my contention by starting in 1956 and citing instances that I thought were "luck" but now see that they are just too numerous and sequential to be just luck. Bear with me, this might get tedious for you but taken as a whole, it is a testament to what the Lord can do for us. In 1956, I met Leroy. Leroy and I were both gun nuts and quickly became close friends. One thing we differed on was what we wanted to do after we graduated. Leroy wanted to join the Marine Corps and I was leaning toward the Air Force because I loved airplanes and my father had been a waist gunner on a B-17 in WWII. Leroy was always talking Marine Corps, but I rarely mentioned the Air Force. We graduated in 1959 and instead of immediately joining the Military, we entered the workforce. I held three jobs by the time 1961 rolled around and was working at General Electric in the Heavy Military Electronics division on the second shift as a janitor but was waiting for an opening in their Apprentice Program. Things were going along quite smoothly. Then, one Friday morning in June, I got a call from Leroy who asked if I would give him a ride into Syracuse because his car wouldn't start. "Sure, where do you need to go?" He told me he was going to the Marine Corps Recruiting Office to sign up. I agreed and into Syracuse, we went. When we got to the Recruiter, he asked me to come in with him since it was warm outside, and he was going to be a while. Into the office, we went.

The recruiter was a Staff Sergeant and he offered me a seat on a couch while he and Leroy discussed what was to happen. While they were talking, I noticed a copy of either "The Marine Corps Gazette" or "Leatherneck", I don't remember which, but I do remember that on the cover was a picture of a Marine wearing the Dress Blue Charlie uniform, standing at Parade Rest in front of an A-4 Skyhawk jet fighter. At about that time, a Staff Sergeant called me and asked if I was thinking about joining the service. I answered yes, I was thinking about joining the Air Force. He then said, "Well, if you would like, you can go take the Armed Forces Qualification Test with your buddy and it will be good for six months and you won't have to take it over. Since I had nothing else to do, this sounded reasonable, and I accepted. We went and took the test.

When we returned to the office, the recruiter was quite excited and told us that we had scored "very high" on the test. He told us that because of our scores, we could be "guaranteed" a position in Marine Corps Aviation. He was careful not to offer any specific job: just that we would be in the Air Wing. Then he asked me if I wanted to go with Leroy and take the Induction Physical since it too would be good for six months if I chose to go into the Air Force. Now, by this time, anyone with any common sense would be hearing alarm bells. I was blissfully ignorant of the physical we went. I should have heard more alarms when they took my blood pressure three times before it was low enough to qualify. Still unaware, we returned to the recruiter.

He then told us that in addition to the aviation guarantee, he could offer us something called the "Buddy Program" which meant we would go through Boot Camp together. He also told us that there were no openings until September, and we wouldn't have to leave until then. Here I present part one of a chain of events that I had erroneously attributed to luck in 2013. Leroy and I left the recruiter as new recruits in the Marine Corps.

That evening Leroy and I went to the Volunteer Fireman's Field Day in North Syracuse. This is a carnival-like event held each year to raise funds for the Fire Department and is like a small carnival. One of the attractions that year was the presence of the winner of the "Miss South Bay Beauty Pageant". South Bay was a smallish town about 20 or so miles north of North Syracuse. "Miss South Bay", the pageant winner, and her court were presented to the attendees of the Field Day and after the presentation, they were free to walk around the grounds. One of Miss South Bay's attendees was a girl that Leroy knew and when they met, he asked her if she would like to go out after Field Day. She said she would, but that Leroy had to find a date for the Queen as they had come together. So, I was to meet Nancy, always referred to as Nan after the initial introduction, and we went out after Field Day. I do not remember much of that night as far as what we did or where we went, but I do know that the two of the most significant events in my life happened that day, joining the Marine Corps and meeting Nan. I didn't know it that night, but Nan and I were to be married a little more than two years later.

On August 30th Leroy and I met at the Recruiting Office and were taken to Albany where we met with several other recruits from around central New York and were given our first set of "orders". For reasons that I still do not understand, I was chosen to carry the orders for all the members of the group, and we were put on a train for New York City. In New York, we changed trains and headed for Savannah Georgia. After a long train ride, we arrived at Yemassee, South Carolina where we got off the train and began our future as United States Marines.

So, what does all of this have to do with 'Devine Intervention?" Basically, it set up the basis for a chain of events that has lasted sixty-one years. Had I not taken Leroy to the recruiter; had I not "impulsively" joined the Marine Corps, I would have never married Nan and my future would have been much different. I was a naïve, overweight, 19-year-old whose life experience up to then was very limited to Central New York, which I supposed was pretty much the same everywhere else. Without reviewing every day of my life, I will try and generally illustrate instances, chronologically, which I had originally written off as "good luck".

After boot camp and Infantry Training which all Marines go through after enlistment, Leroy and I went to Naval Air Station in Millington, Tennessee where the Navy trained Marines and Sailors who were to be in the Naval and Marine Corps aviation units throughout the world. We were first assigned to "Aviation Fundamentals" classes where we learned the basics of how Navy and Marine's squadrons worked and what "jobs" we might be trained for. Briefly, you could opt for working on aircraft engines, electrical systems, airframes, avionics systems, and lastly training devices, and flight simulators. After the introductory course, we were to select which area we wanted to work in. Leroy chose electronics and I, for reasons I do not remember, chose training devices. We graduated from our respective schools and were sent to our first Duty Stations. Leroy and I were both sent to Marine Corps Air Station Cherry Point, North Carolina. There, Leroy was assigned to Marine Aircraft Group 12, and I was assigned to Headquarters and Headquarters Squadron as the flight simulators were not squadron specific but served all the Marine Pilots at Cherry Point.

Nan and I wrote to each other regularly, and I settled into doing a job I really loved. The simulators in those days were not as sophisticated as they would become but were sufficiently representative of the aircraft that I got to be a "pilot" without ever leaving the ground. Not long after working with the devices, I was at the rifle range during annual requalification and heard about some openings on the Air Station Pistol team. I had shot expert with the M-1 but was not required to qualify with the pistol, so I had doubts about my chances but applied for the pistol team anyway since pistol matches were a lot less physically demanding than rifle matches. To my great surprise, I tried it out and was accepted to be on the team. This had several consequences that were to manifest themselves as time passed, but for the moment, I was quite pleased with my daily "duties" which consisted of spending the mornings as a coach for Officers and Staff Non-Commissioned Officers who were required to qualify each year with the pistol, and afternoons shooting the Colt .45 automatic pistol to my heart's content.

One of those unknown consequences came in the Spring of 1963 when the team shooters were ordered to the U.S. Naval Academy in Annapolis, Maryland for two weeks of temporary duty coaching the incoming class of Naval Academy Freshmen as they qualified with the M-1 and the .45. We worked during the week and had weekends off and I came up with the brilliant idea of flying up to New York and spending a weekend with Nan. So, Friday afternoon I took a flight from Annapolis to Syracuse and spent Saturday and Sunday morning with Nan. Sunday found us at Hancock Airport where I was to take my return flight to Annapolis. About thirty minutes prior to the flight, they announced it was canceled for mechanical reasons. When I inquired about the next flight out, I was told it would be Monday morning. This was a big problem, as I would not be able to get back to the range before duty time, effectively becoming AWOL! While I was talking with Nan and our parents, a Sailor came over and said he and two of his friends were also due back at Annapolis and that they were going to drive back to avoid being AWOL and I was welcome to join them. This was too good to be true!

While it seemed like a good deal to me, it did not appeal to our parents or to Nan and I wound up declining the offer. I then placed a call to the Duty Officer at the Range and explained the problem. I was told to get on the earliest possible flight back and report to the Officer-in-Charge of the range detail when I got back. Monday morning, I made the trip back to Annapolis and took a cab to the range. During the ride, the driver had the radio on, and the news was carrying a story about an automobile accident a little North of Annapolis and that three Sailors from Annapolis had been killed. It appeared that they were returning from Syracuse, New York. I sat there, stunned for a moment, and thought, 'Boy, was I lucky that I didn't catch that ride!" Was I "lucky"?

When I reported back to the range, the Officer-in-Charge called me into his office and asked me if I had ever been in trouble before. I said no and he told me that because I had called in and reported to myself that he wasn't going to do anything official about the incident and to get me behind into uniform and back on the firing line. I think I was a little wiser than I had been on the prior Friday. I also learned that I had been promoted to Corporal while we were at Annapolis which was what Nancy and I had agreed would be when we would be able to get married. So, that November, I took leave and went back to Syracuse where Nan and I were married on November 16th, 1963.

We came back to Cherry Point and moved into enlisted housing with a little help from a friend that got us around the waiting list after we had settled in, I went back to work at Station Training where I was assigned to work at the Aviation Physiology Training unit at the Station Hospital. This is where pilots practiced using the ejection seat and experienced high-altitude flying in the low-pressure chamber. My primary duties involved the maintenance of the 6EQ2E Martin-Baker Ejection Seat Trainer. I did preventive maintenance and assisted the

Navy Corpsmen when they were training pilots. The Martin-Baker ejection seat used at this period used a 37-millimeter cartridge to propel the seat out of the aircraft when he activated it by pulling a set of handles above and slightly behind his head. When pulled, the handles pulled out a canvas face shield that covered the pilot's face and triggered the firing mechanism that shot the pilot and seats out of the aircraft.

The training sessions were conducted outside the hospital next to the ambulance garage. The seat was positioned inside a cockpit-like shell and attached to a set of twenty-foot rails which allowed the seat to ride freely up the rails after the firing mechanism triggered and when it stopped, a gearing mechanism engaged to slowly let the seat back down to the cockpit shell. Pilots were required to wear their flight suits and their helmets during the training sessions, and we normally had ten pilots that were trained in each session. I will note here that we had a scheduled training session, a Marine Ordnance Technician would be present to load the 37-millimeter shells into the firing mechanism for each "shot". This involved removing the top of the firing mechanism and the spent cartridge, loading a new cartridge, replacing the top, and re-cocking the firing pin. He then placed a safety pin into the top of the firing mechanism that prevented the seat from firing if the face curtain was pulled out of sequence. There was also a safety slide that would not let the seat fire unless it was pulled back electrically with a solenoid switch that was attached.

The training session was very regimented and went like this: The seat was armed with the cartridge, cocked, and the safety pin inserted. The pin had a lanyard attached which was for the Ordnance Marine to use to remove the pin as the last step of the ejection sequence was reached by the pilot. The Navy Corpsman who was running the session held the solenoid switch as the pilot went through the steps and at the last step before firing was reached, the Corpsman would activate the switch and the Ordnance man would remove the safety pin with the lanyard.

The sequence of events for the pilot was to reduce airspeed, jettison the canopy, pull his feet back to the seat, activate the emergency oxygen system, and then pull the face curtain which fired the seat and catapulted the pilot and seat out of the aircraft. During the training session, the pilot was instructed to touch, but not activate the controls just to ensure he had the sequence correct. During the actual event, when the Corpsman called out "Activate the emergency oxygen", the Corpsman present the solenoid switch and the Marine Ordnance man pulled the safety pin out using the lanyard attached. For some reason, the lanyard was supposed to be 36 inches long, but for as long as I had been assigned to the unit, the lanyard on this seat was about 12 inches long.

During the time I was assigned to the Physiology unit, the Wing Commander had instituted a policy that if a pilot was not "current" in his required training events, which included annual visits to the unit for training which were made part of his official records. It was this policy that prompted a phone call to the Physiology Unit Officer-in-Charge (OIC) from a pilot who had missed his annual training and was possibly in line to lose flight pay. The OIC agreed to have the pilot come to the unit and get the training that day.

Normally, pilots going through the training sessions wore their flight suits and brought their own flight helmets which were fitted to them. Our pilot showed up for the training wearing his regular uniform and without his helmet. We had a helmet at the unit that he was allowed to use which was larger than his own personal helmet and wearing his regular uniform was not going to affect the ejection seat training, so he started the low-pressure chamber exercise.

Part of the maintenance of the ejection seat trainer involved testing the firing mechanism and therefore we had on sight, a case of 37-millimeter cartridges I knew how to operate the firing mechanism, so we did not call for an Ordnance Marine to come to the unit from across the base since there was only going to be one shot. The pilot finished the chamber exercise, and we went out to the seat and began the exercise. It had rained a little overnight and the air was still a little damp, but not so much as to interfere with the training.

While the Corpsman explained the training event, I loaded the cartridge into the firing mechanism, cocked it, and inserted the safety pin. I then took my position beside the trainer and waited while the pilot went through the first phase of the event, touching but NOT activating the controls. However, when he got to the final step, instead of touching the face curtain handles, he pulled them. With the safety pin still in and the Corpsman not activating the safety solenoid, nothing happened.

I believe the pilot was a Captain, and I, with my rather quick temper, which was to influence life-changing events several more times in my life, got very angry and climbed the steps to the pilot, grabbed the face curtain, and reinserted it into its proper place. In my anger, I forgot to re-cock the firing mechanism. This meant that the only thing preventing the seat from firing was the solenoid and the safety pin. What we did not know at the time was that due to the dampness, the solenoid was, for all intents and purposes, "made" or pressed, so the only thing that was holding the firing pin from dropping was the safety pin on its 12-inch lanyard.

The session re-started and when the Corpsman said, "Activate the emergency oxygen", I pulled the lanyard and to everyone's shock, the seat fired before the pilot even touched the face curtain. As the lanyard was as short as it was, the seat ran over my right hand, chopping off the tip of the index finger, tearing a large gouge in the palm, and chopping out a gouge in the area on the top of the hand between the thumb and index finger. I don't remember if I felt pain, but I do remember a tingling sensation as the Corpsman grabbed me and walked us around the corner of the ambulance garage and into the emergency room. I do remember thinking that if the seat had been fired 15 seconds sooner, I would have been hit in the face and probably killed. "Lucky?", I used to think so. You decide.

Meanwhile, the poor pilot who had unexpectedly been shot out of the cockpit and twenty feet up the rails pushed the helmet, which had been pushed down over his eyes, up and discovered that the left side of his uniform was covered in blood and that there was nobody around the seat on the ground. The seat slowly descended back into the cockpit and a Corpsman came out to the seat and helped the rather dazed Captain out of the trainer. For a short time, he thought I might be dead, but was told that I was badly injured but would survive.

There is one more aspect to this event that I will share with you that I thought was "luck", but now believe otherwise. The duty Doctor in the Emergency Room that day later left the Navy and returned to New

Jersey I think, where he opened a practice specializing in reconstructive surgery of hands and feet. After a long recuperation, I was sent back to duty at the Training Office running a desk. They did send me to Typing school, but when the instructor saw my hand, he told me to go back to my office.

Now, I will put down a series of events that ensued from this point on. They are all related in the sense that they were made possible by the set of circumstances that put me where I was at that time. Nan and I had planned on my finishing my four-year tour of duty and then returning to New York where we would resume our lives in the civilian world. This, however, is not exactly what transpired.

One day, while I was at my desk, a Marine came in and asked me if I would like to make an additional fifty dollars a month. Now, in 1964, that was a pretty good amount of money, especially for a Corporal. I asked him what I had to do to get this windfall. He said that our MOS (Military Occupational Specialty), was classified as "critical" and in order to retain Marines in the field, the fifty-dollar bonus was being offered. There was, however, a small catch. I would have to extend my enlistment for two years to qualify. Without even thinking about it, I said yes and signed up for the extension of my enlistment. I then "remembered" that I was a married person and probably should have talked this over with Nan. Surprisingly, when I told her what I had done, she was quite receptive to the idea, and nothing more was said.

A few weeks later, another Marine came into my office and asked me if I would like to go to college, have the Marine Corps pay for it, and when I graduated, get commissioned as an Officer. I asked what I had to do to get this, and I was told that I would have to take a College Equivalency Examination and if I qualified, I would be selected. I said I would be interested and a few days later, I took the required test. I had talked to Nan about his one, and we decided that if I was lucky enough to be selected, she was all for it. After the test, I pretty much forgot about the whole thing.

Now at this point, Nan had become a member of the Non-Commissioned Officer's Wives Club. There was a club for Non-Commissioned Officer's wives, Staff Non-Commissioned Officer's wives, and Officer's wives. It was customary that whenever one of the wives' clubs was having events, they would send a courtesy invitation to the Commanding General's wife. The NCO wives club was having a reception and they chose our quarters for the event. When the time came for the festivities, Nan shooed me out the front door to go visit one of my buddies in the housing area and not get in the way. I was rather surprised when I opened the front door and saw a Staff Car pull up and stop. The reception had a Hawaiian theme, and the General's wife was decked out in a mu-mu and was wearing a floral lei. I later learned that she loved Hawaii and was delighted to attend the reception. Again, by the next day, I had pretty much forgotten about it.

Things had settled into a comfortable routine and Nan, and I were very comfortable with our lives at Cherry Point. I worked very regular hours, we had managed to purchase a used Ford station wagon in which we traveled around Eastern North Carolina, especially the beaches which Nan loved. It seemed that we were on our way to serving out my enlistment and then returning home to New York. Well, it didn't quite work out that way.

One day, I was summoned to the Headquarters and was told that I had received a set of orders for duty in Hawaii. This came as quite a surprise as I hadn't asked for any orders, but I knew that orders are orders. It did cross my mind that Nan and the Commanding General's wife had discussed Hawaii at some length at that reception, but I dismissed that notion. I might have been a bit too skeptical as Nan had always wanted to go to Hawaii, could it be her prayers being answered?

While she was quite happy with the orders, she wasn't too pleased to learn that Marines below the rank of Sergeant were not paid to take dependents with them. However, she quickly accepted the situation and planned to go back to New York and go to work to raise the money for her trip. I did advise her to be sure she got enough for a round-trip fare since we couldn't be 100% sure how long I would be there, but it was normally a two-year assignment. As it turned out, round-trip fare was a very good idea.

So, we loaded up our belongings in the Ford and set off for New York. Nan moved back in with her parents, and I set off for Hawaii. This was in September, and by late November Nan had accumulated enough for the airfare and arrived in Honolulu just before Thanksgiving. We rented a small apartment in Kailua, and I went to work every day on a bus that was popularly called the "Kailua Creeper", and Nan spent as much time as she could on a beach she could get to. We made several trips across the island to Honolulu where we would spend days on the beach at Waikiki and evenings at the International Market Place.

In order to supplant my Corporal's pay, Nan got a job at one of the Marine Corps Exchanges' extension shops which happily was located close to the Training Building where I worked. About seven months into what we supposed would be a two-year event, Nan took delivery of the Navy Times newspaper which was sold at the exchanges. She happened to be glancing through it when she got a glimpse of my name. She read the article which was the announcement of that year's selectees for the Naval Enlisted Scientific Education Program, or NESEP. That "college program" I had signed up for and promptly forgotten about had selected me. Two days or so later, the Squadron Office called me in and told me I had orders to the Naval Training Center in San Diego for a six-week preparatory school for the program. This of course meant that Nan had to pack up and use that round-trip ticket back to New York. She was not pleased, but to her credit, as she always had and always would, accepted the fact and while she was in tears going up the ramp into the plane, I knew she was crying because she was leaving Hawaii.

When I got to the school in San Diego, we were informed that if we were successful and graduated from college, we would have to agree to serve a minimum of two years as an Officer. That, plus the four years of school meant we had to sign up for six years. I called Nan this time and she was fine with it, so I signed on the dotted line. So much for leaving the Corps and going back home. I didn't know it then, but I was on a track that was to be full of surprises and revelations, far in excess of what I was seeing at that time. "On a track"? Who put me on that track and why? Again, you decide.

Prep School was easy, and in the fourth week, we were asked to choose from a list of Colleges and Universities three choices, in order. I chose Penn State, Purdue, and the University of Kansas. Penn State because it was close to home, Purdue because "everybody" said it was "neat", and Kansas because it was one of the top Chemistry schools in the country and I had chosen Chemistry as my major. Well, that year Penn State was not accepting out-of-state students, Purdue was full and so I was ordered to the University of Kansas in Lawrence to begin my studies. The re-enlistment bonus money I received was used to buy our first "new" car, a 1965 Rambler which we drove from New York to Lawrence where we settled into the academic lifestyle quite happily.

I made fairly good progress through the first year of school but found some difficulty in the second year with some of the Chemistry classes I was taking. I got some of the worst grades of my life and was worried about maintaining the required "C" average to stay in the program. However, in other areas, my life was doing much better.

When Nan and I married, we decided not to have children naturally due to some medical issues that made pregnancy risky at best for Nan. We discussed this while in Lawrence and decided to try and adopt a child. We went through all the requirements, home studies, interviews, and the like and we were approved. In November of 1966, Nan got a call from the agency that there was a three-day-old baby girl that was being put up for adoption. We went to the hospital and met with the Social Worker and signed a lot of papers and came home with a wonderful little girl. Life, it seemed, was being very kind to us.

Part of the NESEP program requirements was a six-week Officer Candidate Course at Quantico, Virginia. This was the course that ROTC students with no military experience attended and was very much like a shortened version of Recruit Training at the Marine Corps Recruit Depots. This training was conducted during the summer between our Sophomore and Junior years. So, off I went to Quantico. By this time, I had been promoted to Sergeant, but at Quantico, I was just another "Candidate". The training was very much like recruit training with added twists designed to evaluate an individual's leadership potential as most of those who made it through the training would ultimately become 2nd Lieutenants and likely see combat tours in Viet Nam. It was, in effect, a screening and I will tell you that it worked very, very well.

One of the twists I mentioned involved having each Candidate act in all the leadership positions of a Marine combat platoon. You spent a day as a Squad Leader, a Platoon Sergeant, and a Platoon Commander while the platoon operated in the training exercises. On the day I was made the Platoon Sergeant, we were scheduled to make a forced march to a training area, stay overnight and participate in combat drills the next day.

Now, this was in Virginia, in August, so it was very hot and very humid. We assembled after morning chow and set off on the march to the training area, about five or six miles from the billeting area. One of my primary responsibilities during this march was to ensure that the Candidates maintained their proper distance, front to back, in their squad as we marched. We were all carrying our packs and weapons and the pace was quite fast. Keeping the platoon "closed up" involved my constantly running from front to back as we marched to "motivate" Candidates who were not keeping the required distance from the Candidate in front of them.

When we finally reached the training area and halted, I was well worn out physically since I never was a runner and was pushing the weight standards set by the Corps. As I took my place at the head of the platoon, the real Platoon Commander instructed me to have the platoon set up the two-man tents we would sleep in that night. This was a supposedly well-organized procedure with several steps that were designed to have all the tents when erected, line up in a straight line. I had done this before and knew what could and often did happen when this procedure was used. Each Candidate carried, as part of his pack, a shelter half and a tent pole so that two Candidates would be able to set up a pup tent together which they would share for the night. I gave the required commands to get the platoon in a straight line, two arm lengths between each man. The next command required that each man take his bayonet and insert it into the ground just inside his right instep. Now, I had seen this seemingly foolproof procedure fail before and I decided to make sure that we would have a straight line when we were finished.

I went to the first man in line and placed his bayonet in the ground next to his right instep, then went to the center man and repeated the process and to the last man and repeated it again. I then turned and marched back to the head of the platoon and gave the command "Mark positions, mark!". Each of the remaining Candidates removed their bayonets and inserted them into the ground. So far, so good. I then gave the command "One step backward, March". Each Candidate took a step backward and I expected to see a very straight line of bayonets. I was astonished to see a line of bayonets that looked like a snake. Now, although the differences were not huge, they were quite noticeable.

Now, I am exhausted, I am hot and sweating, and I am angry. I lost any sense of composure I might have had and launched into a tirade of cursing, and arm-waving that was right in keeping with my German Italian heritage. That might have been O.K. but then, about halfway down the line, somebody laughed. That was the straw that broke the proverbial camel's back. I reached behind me and pulled my entrenching tool, a small shovel, out of my pack and started down the line after the laughing boy. He saw me coming and he started running away from me. I realized that I would never catch him, so in a frustrated rage, I threw my entrenching tool at him. It missed. What was not missed was my performance, which both the real Platoon Commander and Platoon Sergeant saw as they came over the hill they had crossed to speak with the Company Commander after assigning me the job of preparing the platoon. Not much was said about the incident then, but when we got back to the barracks, I was told I was to have an evaluation board the next day.

I called Nan that night and talked things over with her and she told me to do whatever I thought was best. I knew what to expect from the board and I was not to be disappointed. I reported to the Company Office the next morning and was ushered into a room where there was a single chair sitting about six feet in front of a table where the Company Commander, the Platoon Commander, the Company Sergeant Major, and a Major that I did not know sat facing the chair. I marched in, made a right face, and reported to the board. I was ordered to take a seat and the questioning began. Each member asked me three or four questions, then passed them to the next man. I knew that there was only one question that was going to be asked that was of any importance, and it would come last. When all the members had finished, the Company Commander asked that question. "Candidate, do you still want to be a Marine Corps Officer?"

I need to add at this point that before I left Kansas for Quantico, I was told I had been selected for promotion to Staff Sergeant. This wasn't critical to my response, but it did add a little bit of comfort to me when I responded. "No Sir".

This was, of course, not the answer the board was expecting, and I knew that if I had answered in the affirmative, I would have been "counseled" and then sent back to finish the training cycle. I had thought long and hard the night before and I knew that if I were to eventually be commissioned, I would likely find myself in the Vietnam Conflict, in charge of combat Marines. If that were to happen in a combat situation, the odds were, in my belief, a loss of self-control such as that at the training area, would almost certainly lead to Marines being killed or wounded because of me.

The board members were visibly taken aback by my answer, and finally, the Company Commander said, "I'll give you credit Candidate for your honesty, but can you tell why?" I simply answered that I did not think I would be a "Good Marine Officer". After an awkward pause, I was told I was dismissed and that I would have to see the Battalion Commander the next day.

The next day, I reported to the Battalion Commander who asked me a few more questions, then the important, "Do you still want to" question." I gave him the same answer I had given the board. He also commented on my honesty and told me to go back to the Company area, pack my gear and wait on a set of orders back to Kansas.

At this time, there is absolutely no way to determine what outcome my being commissioned would have created, but I still believe that I made the right decision and now I realize I likely had some intervention, and I am very thankful for that.

I reported back to Kansas and was ordered to report to Marine Corps Air Station, Beaufort, South Carolina, and was promoted to Staff Sergeant. We packed up our belongings and set out for Beaufort. My goal of attaining a degree seemed to be truncated. But things sometimes are not as they seem.

Life at Beaufort was quite pleasant, we had comfortable quarters, I was back working on flight simulators, we were close enough to visit Savanah, Georgia, and Charleston, South Carolina, and Nan had been reunited with a friend she had made in Hawaii, the wife of a Gunnery Sergeant that I had met in Tennessee and then again in Hawaii. He was now working at the Training Building with me. Things were going along nicely when I got a call from the Squadron Office. It seemed that somewhere along the line, I had applied to attend TD- "B" School, an advanced course taught at Millington. I had totally forgotten about it, but there it was, so we packed up and reported to Millington, Tennessee for "Duty Under Instruction". This was a bonus for Nan as her parents had moved to Jackson Tennessee where her dad had been sent to work. We visited nearly every weekend with them, and everyone was quite content. When I graduated from "B" School, I was ordered to Marine Corps Air Station, El Toro in California. We loaded up once again and drove to California and the next chapter of our lives.

California was very different from any place we had lived in up to that point. We had to have Nan stay with her parents until I was assigned government housing because the rents were so high in the Santa Ana area. It took about five weeks before we were able to have Nan and our daughter return and move into quarters aboard the base. Southern California was quite a departure from what we had been used to, but it wasn't all bad.; there was Disneyland.

While we were in California, the Sergeant Major of the Marine Corps visited the base and was promoting a new program the Marine Corps had initiated, the Staff Non-Commissioned Officer's Degree Completion Program. Staff NCOs with two years of college could apply and if accepted, attend a college of their choice and complete their degree requirements. There was no restriction as to what area of study was concerned, the Corps wanted to have more Staff NCOs with a degree. Without giving it a lot of thought, I put in an application. Naturally, I was among the 50 Marines chosen in the first year. What school did I choose? Kansas University of course. However, I changed my course of study from Chemistry to Geography. I had been exposed to that course of study while I was in NESEP and some of the Marines there were majoring in that. I was not to regret the decision. So, in the late summer of 1972, we packed up and returned to Lawrence, Kansas. Luck? Coincidence? Fate? Something else… you decide.

The next two years were very pleasant and easy. I found the curriculum quite interesting and appealing, and I was able to maintain my grades well enough to protect my continued enrollment. During those two years, I learned that my Training Device MOS was going to be retired and that the Marines holding the MOS would be reassigned to compatible MOSs wherever possible. So, when I finally reached completion of my studies and was to be graduated, I called HQMC to see what new MOS I would be assigned to.

I told the Monitor that I was graduating. I asked if it might be logical to assign me to an Intelligence or meteorology-based MOS where I could use the training I had just completed. I was told that the technical aspects of my MOS were considered "critical" as were most of the Aviation Electronics assignments and that I would be assigned as a Test Equipment Calibration and Repair Specialist. Then I was told that I would be sent from KU to Iwakuni, Japan after my graduation. I told the Monitor that I would be reporting as a Senior Staff Non-Commissioned Officer to a unit whose work I was only vaguely familiar with and requested an assignment where I would not be as senior, and I could learn the MOS requirements. Surprisingly, I was sent to Marine Corps Air Station, Cherry Point, North Carolina for one year before I would be ordered to Iwakuni. This was to have some very profound effects on not only my life but on Nan and Mara as well.

Cherry Point was to be a very happy and important part of my future. I was assigned to the Precision Measuring Equipment (PME) shop in Marine Corps Combat Readiness Training Group 20 (MCCRTG-20) which was housed in one of the hangars adjacent to the flight line at Cherry Point. I spent only a year there, during which an AV-8 Harrier aircraft crashed close to the hangar I was assigned to and slid through the hangar, on fire until it stopped in the parking lot on the other side. Amazingly, while the pilot did not survive the event, no other personnel were injured. In fact, we were on leave in South Carolina visiting Nan's parents prior to my assignment to Japan. There was that "good luck" thing again??

Once my year of familiarization was complete, I was off to Japan. We decided to have Nam and Mara stay in Columbia, South Carolina with her parents while I was in Japan. Here I will share some advice.

When facing a very long flight over a large part of the Pacific Ocean, don't read a book like "Jaws". It was a long flight, and I was very, very uncomfortable. I secretly hoped that if there was a problem that the aircraft would explode rather than go down in the Ocean. It didn't do either and I eventually found myself in Iwakuni, Japan assigned to the Marine Aircraft Group 12 PME shop. My time in Japan was a very interesting one. I learned that the Japanese people were very polite and industrious people. They worked hard and they played hard.

The thirteen months at Iwakuni passed, more slowly than I would have liked, but they passed. I would usually spend my off time at the Staff NCO Club eating dinner and playing on the slot machines which were there. I quickly learned that I was addicted to those one-armed bandits and even though the maximum amount you could bet was a quarter, you could spend quite a bit in a short period of time. I didn't want to lessen the amount of money I was sending home to Nan at her parent's home in South Carolina, so I started looking for some sort of work to offset my habit.

While I was at the Staff NCO Club one evening, two civilian gentlemen came in. The club, as usual, was quite busy and they were looking for seats. I was sitting alone and invited them to join me. It turned out that they were reporters from the "Stars and Stripes" newspaper. During our conversation, they learned that I had a College Degree. They happened to know that the United States Armed Forces Institute, USAFI, was looking for degreed personnel to teach night classes to Marines who did not have a High School Diploma but had a GED instead. They asked me if I would be interested, and I said yes. While my degree was in Geography, I wound up teaching American History and found it extremely rewarding as well as financing my gambling affliction. I am quite certain that I learned more than any of the Marines I taught, but it was very satisfying for students who really wanted to learn.

About the third week of the class, the reporters showed up and asked if they could sit in on the class. I noticed one of them had a camera with him and I agreed to their joining the group. To this day I don't think I can remember a word I said that night, but it must have been good enough for the reporters as there was an article in the next edition of the paper. Yes, I still have a copy. This was my first experience in working with "teaching" groups and I found it quite satisfying. It was also quite prophetic. That "luck" thing again?

The remaining time I spent in Iwakuni was uneventful, and I received orders to Return to Cherry Point. At Cherry Point, we were assigned to Military Housing on the Base and were quite comfortable. I was assigned to Mobile Calibration Complex 2 (MCC-2), a van complex much like the one in Iwakuni. Our function was to calibrate and repair all the electronic test equipment used by all the Second Marine Aircraft Wing squadrons assigned to Cherry Point. The duty was satisfying, and I was comfortable, all things were going well.

It was then that we met two remarkable Marine Corps families. Up to this point, we had not forged any strong ties with other Marines and their families because we had spent so much time away from Marine Corps installations. It was 1975 and we were to spend the balance of my military career at Marine Corps Air Station Cherry Point, Marine Corps Air Station New River, and Marine Corps Base, Camp Lejeune, all along the Eastern Coast of North Caroline within 50 miles of each other.

The first family lived near us in housing aboard the Air Station. Bob's wife Kathy happened to be a Girl Scout Troop Leader. Mara had been in the Brownies while living with Nan's parents in South Carolina and was eager to move up to the Girl Scouts. The moment Nan and Kathy met, there was an immediate attraction and they remained fast friends until Nan's passing, even though they had moved back to Minnesota in the 80s. Nan was asked and agreed to be the Assistant Troop Leader. They had three children and Kathy's husband Bob worked at the Nuclear, Biological, and Chemical (NBC) School. Bob and I also became close, and we all spent a considerable amount of time together. One of Bob's friends at the NBC School was another Bob, whose wife was nicknamed Suki from their time in Okinawa. The group formed and has endured to this day, though Nan, of course, is waiting on us in Paradise. We shared good times, bad times, and all other times and still communicate today though Suki and Bob are in Pennsylvania, Kathy and Bob are in Minnesota and I remain in North Carolina.

When I first joined the Corps, I was, as I said, overweight and not physically inclined. In Boot Camp, I became much more physically fit and had no problems meeting fitness requirements as they were monitored. That situation prevailed until I graduated from the University of Kansas. The Marine Corps had made several changes to physical fitness standards and the resulting requirements were to prove very difficult for me. The biggest challenge was the three-mile run. During the time prior to this, Marines were required to perform a three-mile march, with helmet, marching pack, and rifle in 36 minutes or less. While it was strenuous for me, I could manage the test within the allotted time. The standard was changed to a three-mile run in 30 minutes. The run was made in physical training gear, sneakers, gym shorts, and shirts. While the 6-minute difference may seem to be sufficient to offset the helmet, pack, uniform, and rifle, no matter how hard I tried, I was unable to complete the run under the time limit. I had been a smoker since the age of 16 and I initially thought that I couldn't make the run because I would "run out of air".

As was the current policy, failing the test meant you would be assigned to "remedial" physical training, usually conducted daily in the morning where we would perform the other required exercise, then finish with the run. This went on for some time and I could not see any improvement in my performance. I knew that my next Fitness Report would reflect a failure of the test and was a serious deterrent to a career. I went to the Naval Hospital and saw a doctor, hoping he might be able to provide some help. After relating the problem to him, he determined that the trouble was, "You are overweight and a smoker".

Putting this counsel into action, I quit smoking and lost about ten pounds in a month. The result? I still could not make the run. I would make the halfway point and on the return run, I would lose strength in my legs, and by the time I reached the starting point again, I could barely stand until I rested for five minutes or longer. I went back to the Doctor and explained these events and he responded, "You are overweight and a smoker"!

This cycle went on for several months and I soon found myself nearing the end of my term of enlistment. As a Gunnery Sergeant unable to pass the Physical Fitness Test, I knew that I would not be allowed to enlist and would be returned to Civilian Life with 17 years of service, 3 years short of retirement. No pay, no benefits, nothing. I was at a loss as to what I should do.

It was at this time that Nan suggested that since the military medical system wasn't helping, I should see a civilian doctor. I told her that we weren't supposed to use civilian medical help. She looked me straight in the eyes and said, "So what will they do, discharge you"? Feeling a little silly, I agreed, and we set up an appointment at Duke Medical Center.

On the day of the appointment, I saw a doctor and explained the problem. He nodded, thought for a minute then asked me to lie on the examination table. He took out his stethoscope and listened to my legs. Then he had me stand back up and run in place for about thirty seconds. Then he sent me to the X-Ray department. They X-Rayed my legs and returned me to the waiting area. About twenty minutes later the Doctor called me back into his office.

He told me he knew what the problem was, it wasn't smoking or weight, it was Peripheral Vascular Disease. During exercise, the blood flow in my legs was diminished by calcium deposits in the veins and that allowed lactic acid to build up and cause the muscles to lose strength. I got a written diagnosis and we returned to Cherry Point. The next day, I took the information to the Naval Hospital and asked to see the doctor who had been treating me, I expected that he might dismiss the information from Duke as it was not "from proper authority". I was told that that doctor had been transferred and I would be seeing his replacement. I wonder about the timing of these events, but you decide.

When the new doctor found out what I wanted was his endorsement of the information, he looked at it and said, "This is from Duke!" To shorten this adventure, I will just say that I received a medical endorsement on my records, I was given a pass on the running portion of the Physical Fitness Test and from then on, I would be given a "Partial Pass" on the test as I could perform the other events with no trouble. When my next fitness report went to Headquarters Marine Corps, it had a "Partial Pass" notification. Shortly thereafter, I was granted re-enlistment and signed up for my next four years. Lucky? I don't know.

Not long after this adventure, another issue arose that was to have, as you may expect, "unforeseen outcomes". Our daughter had a learning disability that made school a formidable challenge for her and up until this time, she had managed to cope with the issue as she was in civilian schools that gave her appropriate assistance. Cherry Point did not have a school on base, and she was attending the county school. For the first time, she was not provided with the assistance she needed and was not doing well. I forget how we learned about the Base Schools at Camp Lejeune and New River but when we found out, I applied for a humanitarian transfer to New River where she would receive appropriate assistance. In short order, I was ordered to Marine Corps Air Station, New River.

There was one other occurrence during this time that might be considered luck, but again, I leave it up to you. I had been very lucky during the years promotion-wise. I had been promoted to Private First-Class during Infantry training at Camp Geiger. I later learned that the reason I was selected was that the Marine on the list ahead of me was caught sleeping during an instruction class. That was 1961. Then I was promoted to Meritorious Lance Corporal when I graduated from Training Devices Class "A" at Millington because I was the Class Honor man. That was 1962. I was made Sergeant in 1965, Staff Sergeant in 1967and Gunnery Sergeant in 1969. Then the PFT course arose, and I didn't make Master Sergeant until 1979, coincidentally right after the first fitness report with a Partial Pass on the PFT arrived at Headquarters. More good luck? As I related at the beginning of this journey through time, I was told that all the running I was required to do before I was diagnosed with that circulation problem probably saved my life in 1986 after my heart attack. One might say that "He works in mysterious ways". You decide if that is true, or if it was just luck.

We made our way to Jacksonville, and I was issued temporary quarters on Camp Jejeune where our daughter entered the base school system. We were quite pleased with the school and things quickly got better for our daughter. I commuted to and from the housing area named Tarawa Terrace to the Air Station at New River. I found my job quite satisfying and thoroughly enjoyed the area and my wife was quite happy to be closer to the beaches, which we visited frequently. Life, in general, was going quite well.

My assignment at New River was as the Non-Commissioned Officer in Charge, NCOIC, of the Test Equipment shop in Headquarters and Maintenance Squadron Twelve (H&MS-12) which was part of Marine Corps Aircraft Group Twenty-Nine (MAG-29). The work was satisfying and the Marines who worked with me were all able and willing performers. The days came and went with little or no problems and I was quite content, as were Nan and our daughter. After about three months, we were moved from Tarawa Terrace to SNCO housing on the Air Station, and our daughter was assigned to the base school there which was as good or better than the one at Camp Lejeune.

At this point, I feel it is time to explain the rest of this story if you will. I have previously cited some examples that sufficiently gave people a reason to ask if there was a question as to whether there might have been some force or reason that the results of the events turned out as they did or that it was nothing more than fortunate circumstances. I believe that the outcomes were instances of intervention by a greater power, i.e., the Lord. You may believe otherwise. However, from here on, other than my recovery from the heart attack in 1986, the events that transpired might seem to be quite normal or expected.

What makes me believe that they were also influenced as part of a plan that was worked out for me beginning on the day I was born? There is a Christian belief that your life is a gift from the Lord, and as such, he directs events, happenings, and outcomes and causes your behavior to reflect that plan. I began this documentation of my life as reflected by events in 1961. Looking at it from that perspective, what might or might not have happened over the course of the next fifty-two years all rests on a phone call from a friend on a Friday morning in June. Had the call not been made; would I be writing this story today?

When I came to the acceptance that there was indeed a Power guiding my thoughts and behaviors, I learned from reading the Bible that the Lord has our best interests at heart if we accept certain rules and behaviors, the most recognizable being the Ten Commandments.

If we try to follow those rules, we are said to be "Blessed". If we do not follow them, we are taking our chances. We are also allowed to make mistakes and if we sincerely "apologize", we are forgiven. This is all very basic and invites serious philosophical debate and people argue back and forth all the time. Basically, there are believers and non-believers; there is that choice. There are also those who have little or no knowledge of the concept. I will not attempt any further Biblical "teaching" as I do not feel qualified. Rather, from here on, I will chronicle significant life events and I believe that I have been truly blessed. Can I be 100% certain that the Lord brought me along the route? I will answer yes but that is based on my faith in the existence of the Lord. Not everyone will agree. But, at the end of the story, I think that some, maybe many, will agree. We shall see.

When I reported to New River, I noticed that there was a building that housed Helicopter Flight Simulators. My last time working on simulators was in the early 70s at Marine Corps Air Station, El Toro California. I worked on simulators for the KC-130 and the CH-46 Helicopter. This was my first experience with helicopter flying and as the simulators were not yet advanced enough, I found flying the device a challenge as they did not use the same control systems as fixed-wing aircraft. That did not stop me from visiting the site whenever I could, and I got to know all the Civil Service workers there. There was a simulator for the CH-46 and the CH-53D and whenever the opportunity presented itself, I would get in and learn how to fly the aircraft.

At this time, the Marine Corps was procuring a simulator for the new CH-53E helicopter, a "bigger and better" version of the CH-53D. This was to prove to be very fortunate for me. I was quite happy with New River, my job, and life in general. I was also nearing the end of my current enlistment and would have to decide whether I should re-enlist or leave active duty with 20 years of service. This would entitle me to retirement pay and benefits for life. There was, however, something involved in this decision that made it anything but simple. First, if I did re-enlist, I would probably make Master Gunnery Sergeant, the top enlisted grade, but I would also very probably be given another overseas assignment for a year. That did not appeal to me at all, and I was not even close to sorting the question out.

One afternoon in 1981, I was visiting the simulator building and talking with the Civilian Supervisor. He mentioned that the contract for the new CH-53 simulator had been accepted and that delivery of the device was scheduled soon. He also told me that they would have to add to the Civil Service staff and that with my prior simulator experience, I had a very good chance of being hired. That information tipped the scales for me, and I put in the paperwork to be retired from active duty in September. Within two weeks the paperwork was returned and accepted, and I began preparing to move to civilian life.

I visited the simulator building and told the supervisor what I had done, and he told me that there had been some "slippage" in the delivery date for the device and therefore, hiring additional staff would be delayed. This was somewhat problematic as I had not attempted to find any work to augment my retirement pay. I was assured I would be notified when I could apply for the position at the simulator building, and while not a promise. I was certain I would be hired.

My retirement ceremony came and after the customary retirement ceremony on the apron in front of the hangar, I slid into the civilian world. We rented a very nice home on the outskirts of Jacksonville with an option to buy. It sat on two acres and had two outbuildings that were built as workshops for the owner who was an Electrician by trade. This was to prove to be quite a convenience later.

While were stationed at Cherry Point, our daughter would visit the riding stables that were aboard. There, she met a large, black thoroughbred and there was an immediate bond between them. After we had moved to New River, we would usually find time each weekend to go back up the Cherry Point and let our daughter ride "her" horse. Not long before I left active duty, I got a call from my wife who asked me if we could buy a horse. Buy a horse? It seemed that the stables at Cherry Point were not doing well financially and were going to close. This, of course, required the horses to be sold. It so happened that our frequent regular visits to the stables went not unnoticed, and they called and wanted to know if we wanted to buy the horse our daughter had grown to love. As the horses were sold at a silent auction, we were told how much to bid and were rewarded with the news that we now owned "her" horse. When we moved to Camp Lejeune, they also had a stable and our daughter became a "regular" and we got to know all the staff and many other families that rode there. In addition, they had a private barn where Marine families could board horses. When we got the call, we were totally unprepared to go collect the horse and bring him down to Lejeune, but a visit to the stable's office produced a volunteer transporter and we rented a stall in the private barn.

We did not tell our daughter about any of this, and the horse arrived in early December. The Stable staff took care of all his needs. As they did for all the animals there, and we waited until Christmas Day when we suggested we go to the stables and take some cookies to the staff that was working there to wish them a Merry Christmas. Never one to turn down a visit to the stables our daughter who was now 15 years old, gladly agreed. Once there, we asked the office where we might find a particular Groom that knew us. We ere told he was out in the Private barn. We walked to the barn, a large building with stalls on both sides and a wide aisle between them. We went in and walked down the aisle with our daughter trailing us, looking at all the horses. About halfway down the aisle, our daughter shouted out to us, "Mom! Dad! Look, it's Cougar! Somebody bought Cougar!" We turned around and told her that yes, someone did buy him, we did, and he is now yours. I can still hear her joyous scream as she went to him and hugged him. I don't think we ever topped that Christmas present.

Time moved along and eventually; I was hired as a Civil Servant at the simulator building. The job title was Integrated Electronic Systems Mechanic. By this point in time, the simulator technology had advanced to the point that the devices faithfully duplicated the responses of the aircraft to the actions of the pilot, there was a hydraulic motion system that made the occupants "feel" that they were "flying" and there was an added visual system that depicted visually what the pilot would be seeing in the real aircraft.

As the simulators became more and more technical, it was realized that the "instructor", an actual helicopter pilot, was hard-pressed to both instruct the student pilot and operate the complicated Instructor's console. Before the devices moved into the Civil Service realm, the instructor pilots were assisted by one of the enlisted maintenance personnel who would operate the instructor console to create the condition the instructor pilot wanted. This had two serious drawbacks; one, the instructor pilots had to tell the maintenance man what situation he wanted to create which was easily heard by the Student Pilots, thereby negating the ability to gauge the pilots' attentiveness and awareness of developing problems. In addition, actual pilots were not happy to be put "in the box"; they much rather wanted to be flying the actual aircraft. By the time I was added to the staff at New River, there was another group of Civil Servants that were formal aviators and acted as instructors. There was a syllabus created and students would fly one-hour "hops" with one of the instructors creating situations and conditions that the actual aircraft might experience and watching the pilots react and record the results for later review.

There were a total of 29 instructors and maintenance personnel assigned to the staff and we worked in three shifts. The day shift and the afternoon shifts were primarily instructors with one or two maintenance personnel to respond to minor functional issues with the devices and the Midnight shift performed all preventive maintenance procedures and repaired functional problems that had arisen during the day that were too complex to be easily repaired. We grew to be quite complimentary and effective as a group. I thought I had found what I would be spending the rest of my working life doing right here at the simulator building. As it turned out, fate, chance, or intervention was to intervene, albeit not right away.

From 1982 on, life was virtually something I reveled in. I especially liked the Midnight shift where I was assigned to the new CH-53E simulator. When we started the shift, we would review a document termed "The Yellow Sheet". It was virtually the same document that was used for the real aircraft where pilots would note any mechanical problems or issues for the maintenance personnel to correct. For us, if there were no problems reported, we were too "pre-flight" the simulator by flying it and looking for issues that needed attention. I would usually take off from New River, fly down to the civilian airport at Wilmington, do a touch and go landing, then fly back up to the air station at Cherry Point, do another touch and go, then fly back to New River and land. To be truthful, it was like playing the most expensive video game in the world and getting well paid for it.

In 1985, two of the other maintenance technicians and I decided we would open a computer maintenance shop in town and repair computers for the civilians. We rented a small store and opened it. At this time, the civilian world was being introduced to Commodore 64 and we thought that we could offer repairs at a much cheaper rate than those sites that would replace entire assemblies rather smaller defective components in the assemblies. This, in theory, made perfect sense. What we had not considered was the extremely delicate work that required removing the smaller components and replacing them. The work required unsoldering and resoldering the smaller component and it was extremely easy to damage the assembly in the process. Despite that challenge, we soldiered on, and much of my spare time was spent at the shop. After a few months, revenues were small, and profits even smaller. It was decided to move the shop to the garage of one of the owners.

After about two or three weeks, we moved the equipment to the garage and were back in business. We struggled but were determined to make a go of it. It was on a Saturday morning when while working on a computer, I began experiencing chest pain, then difficulty breathing. My partner drove me to the Hospital and in short order, I was airlifted to Duke where they performed a 5-vessel coronary artery graft. After the surgery, the doctors told me that because I had done so much running in the Corps, my heart had created its own bypasses around blockages. Those bypasses essentially saved my life by giving the surgeons time to remove the newer blockages. Was I "lucky" again?

Thus ended my venture into the business world as it were and after I had recuperated, I returned to the simulator building. The next few years went along quite smoothly, and I was anticipating that I would eventually retire from this position. Once again, I was surprised when fate, luck, or intervention created a new adventure.

In the 1980's The Department of the Navy embarked on a program of comparing the cost of operating its bases and stations with having the work performed by civilian contractors. This was an attempt to reduce operating costs and Improving performance. As the Marine Corps is part of the Department of the Navy, Marine Corps installations were included in the program. Under a process called A-76, the outcomes of these studies were what was called the Government Cost Estimate (GCE). The installation costs were studied to determine what processes were required to meet the operational requirements and a document was created called the Statement of Work (SOW). This was then analyzed to determine the cost required to perform the work described. This SOW would be provided to potential bidders who would work up their estimate of the costs required to meet them. The in-place workforce would also create an estimate of their cost which was termed the Government Cost Estimate (GCE). Once the bidders had made their proposals, they would be compared to the GCE, and the lowest cost would "win". As we were the smallest Marine Corps Air Station in the Corps, we were the last to be studied and, as all the others had lost out to contractors, we were not very hopeful of the results.

The installation function that was to create our GCE was the Management Assistance Office, (MAO). They assigned two Management Analysts to perform the study and required a member of the workforce to be assigned to the team to aid. For whatever reason, I was assigned to be that member. This study was only conducted for the maintenance force as the instructors were exempted.

We began the analysis and in about two weeks, we had determined the GCE. Since New River was so small, the contractor bidding process was eliminated and the SOW was analyzed by an analyst from the Naval Training Systems Headquarters in Orlando, Florida. He visited the unit for a few days and then returned to Orlando. About two days after he had returned, we were informed that the GCE was lower than the estimated contractor costs and we would not be contracted. Lucky? Fate?, Intervention? You decide.

While the fact that we would not be contracted was good news, there was a problem that our cost estimate created. We had made our estimate based on the absolute minimum number of maintenance employees required. In a nutshell, this meant that we would have to reduce the workforce to that number. This would require letting four employees go. This would create a very complicated and tedious condition. For Civil Servants who are released under these conditions, if you are terminated without cause, a process called "Bump and Retreat" is initiated. This means if you are senior to and/or have more or the same amount of service time than an equivalent employee, you can "bump" them and assume their position. This covers the entire installation and is a very big headache. For this reason, it was decided that instead of the Bump and Retreat, the installation would just find other jobs suitable to their abilities. For whatever reason, I was assigned to the MAO, as they felt I had the skills required while assisting them in creating the SOW. So, One Friday I left New River as an Integrated Systems Mechanic and came back to work Monday as a Management Analyst.

When I left active duty, we were no longer able to board Cougar on the base. Fortunately, there was a private stable not far from our home where we were able to board him. It was here that I met a young man who was doing Ferrier work for the stable. He and our daughter got along very well and when he and I met, there was an immediate bond, and he became a familiar presence with the whole family. We eventually moved Cougar to our home after I built a stall out of one of the outbuildings. At the time we moved in, the home was surrounded by farmland, and the lot we were on had a full acre of land in front which I fenced in and turned into pasture for Cougars. I also rented another acre of pasture on the west side of our lot. Cougar seemed to be quite content with the arrangement and when our daughter wasn't in school, she was caring for or riding Cougar around the area. It would appear that we had, at last, found our final resting spot after years of moving about every two years.

My move to the MAO was to prove extremely interesting and quite educational. The MAO was primarily responsible for ensuring the Installation was following all the various Instructions, Orders, and guidelines issued by higher headquarters. One of the primary examples of this was the Department of the Navy's 'Efficiency Review" (ER) program. This program mandated that all the functional areas of the command would be regularly reviewed to determine if there might be ways to lower costs and or improve performance. The MAO would gather all the appropriate regulations, Instructions, Standard Operating Procedures, and any other guidelines the Function Under Study (FUS) operated under. We would analyze the documentation while observing the daily activities as they were performed. We would also interview individuals working within the function for any ideas they might provide. If we find anything that might improve in any way the function's performance, we will create a proposal to implement any changes that might be made. The proposal would be given to the Director of the function for comments and endorsements. The proposal would then be passed to the Commanding Officer who would either accept or reject proposed changes and order those that were accepted to be instituted.

I spent several happy years with MAO and learned a multitude of new procedures, methods, and processes which I enjoyed a great deal. I also met most of the civilian employees in the workforce and became quite familiar with how the Air Station operated on a day-to-day basis. Again, I did not know how advantageous this body of knowledge would become.

In 1998, the Head of the MAO retired, and I was selected as her replacement. By this time, there were two other employees that had worked at the simulator building on the staff working with me. It was a very enjoyable organization, and everyone seemed to be very content. Over time, we headed up several Department of the Navy initiatives, all of which were designed to reduce operating costs and improve effectiveness. They had very technical sounding names, Total Quality Leadership (TQL) and Activity Based Costing (ABC), are examples.

A part of all these initiatives was the introduction of a three-day workshop where Air Station personnel would be taught "The 7 Habits of Highly Effective People", The information taken from the very successful book of the same name written by Stephen Covey. I was among the first group from the Air Station to attend a workshop and I found the content extremely interesting. The Air Station then sent me and another Supervisor to a three-day "Facilitators Course" in Washington, DC. We were then tasked with "facilitating" workshops at our installation to expose as many employees as possible. We would ask twenty employees to attend a three-day workshop and share the material with them. Here I will tell you that this assignment while being veryinteresting to me, changed my personality. Prior to this assignment, I was what you might call a Type "A" person. I had a very short temper, and when something went wrong or not as I had anticipated, I would fly into a rage and blame anything or anybody in sight. I remember one incident at the Simulator Building where if one of the supervisors had not intervened in one of my tantrums, I would have physically assaulted another employee. If I had done that, my Civil Service career would have been over. In addition, my family as well as more than a few people have told me that I was a different person after working with this material. He does work in mysterious ways.

As New River was the smallest of the Air Stations, the civilian staff was under three hundred people. This meant the highest-paid positions were limited in number. The GS schedule went from I to 15, and the highest grade at New River was GS-13 held by three individuals. I was a GS-12 and there were quite a few of us, but at all the other installations, those holding the same position were all GS-13s. I understood that I was, for intents and purposes, at my terminal grade. So, I thought.

In the early 2000s. The Marine Corps consolidated its commands geographically. This resulted in the creation of Marine Corps Installations, East, or MCIEAST which consisted of Marine Corps Air Station Cherry Point, Marine Corps Base Camp Lejeune, Marine Air Station Beaufort, and Marine Corps Air Station Quantico. The command was Headquartered at Camp Lejeune and was headed up by a General Officer from the ground command and a Colonel from the Air wing. As it happened, our Commanding Officer was nearing the end of his tour at New River and was assigned to be the MCIEAST Executive Officer.

After about a year, I applied for and was accepted by the Camp Lejeune Business Performance Office as a GS-13. It was a monetary decision since the higher grade would mean a larger retirement check. While this was a positive outcome, I soon realized that there was another dimension I had not taken account of. At New River, we were very much a large family. Everyone knew well everyone else. There was an atmosphere of harmony and while the Chain of Command was adhered to, it was much more congenial in nature. For instance, if I needed to talk to the Commanding Officer, I would walk to the other end of our building, stick my head in the receptionist's office and ask if he was in. If he was, I would walk right in, and we would discuss whatever issue it was and I would walk out. It was customary that I would stick my head into my supervisor's office on the way to the CO's office to let him know I was going, and he would simply nod and go back to what he was doing.

At Camp Lejeune, which was six or seven times larger, I soon found out that if I wanted to talk to my Supervisor, a GS-15, I first had to call my 'first-line supervisor a GS-14, to get permission. The atmosphere at Lejeune was very, very stiff and formal. Only within our small office was the family-like atmosphere and even that was somewhat stiffer. I tried my best to adjust to this but never really felt as much a part of the bigger picture as I did a New River.

Once acclimated, I settled in, and with a staff of very capable and willing associates, we proceeded to attend to the duties at hand. There were some interesting challenges and processes for the staff, and we did what I thought was excellent management. Then came the proverbial "straw" that broke the camel's back. My direct assistant was extremely competent and very eager to please. She was really doing the work of two people cheerfully and doing it well. The Navy Department had instituted a new personnel system which was quite hard to adapt to and manage. Part of the program provided a process whereby a supervisor could submit a recommendation to award a performance-based pay increase to a deserving employee. I wrote my assistant a recommendation and forwarded it "up the chain" as it were. I fully expected it to be approved quite quickly. So much for expectation. I was playing golf on a day off when I got a phone call from my GS-15 Supervisor informing me that they were having a board to review these references from the department and that they did not feel I had "fully justified" my recommendation and therefore it was being rejected. To my credit, and thanks to my new "attitude", I chose not to lose control and simply acknowledged the call. The next day, I began searching for another position on the base.

It was about a week later I got a call from the Naval Hospital for an interview to fill an Analyst position in their business office. I went to the interview and while I was answering questions, I explained that I was considering retirement in about two years. I was sure that I had made my selection for the position quite remote. Not so. I got a call saying I had been selected for the job. My supervisor wasn't very happy with the short notice but didn't have any way of stopping me from accepting, which I did.

The job was similar in many respects to what I had been doing for a long time but had some specific elements that I had not been exposed to. The most important of these was becoming familiar with the HIPPA constraints associated with the medical services provided by the hospital. I was given several written orders and other documents which I worked my way through and felt comfortable with the concept. The work was in the Finance Office of the hospital, and I was immediately accepted as part of the well-organized and quite pleasant staff.

About a month after I had started working, I was called into the Supervisor's office where I was given a list of training and educational courses I would be attending. I contemplated this somewhat unexpected news and realized that if I accepted this course of training events, I would have felt obligated to stay in the position much longer than I had planned. I reminded the Supervisor of my intent to retire and asked that I be retained only as long as it took to find another Analyst. She accepted my request and in 2009, I submitted my retirement request and left the Service to the Government. It had been a remarkable journey and I was quite proud of my record.

By now, having read through this somewhat lengthy depiction of events, you are probably wondering what has all this to do with Intervention by the Lord. Admittedly, there were a few instances that were easily associated with possible interventions. There was the training accident that nearly ended my life, the trip back to Annapolis that I didn't take, and the heart attack that I survived because of all the running that I hated. There are also several instances that most people would chalk up to "good luck" or "fate". While I cannot offer undeniable facts or other proof that Intervention was responsible, I am convinced that without the help of the Lord, I wouldn't be sitting here in North Carolina writing this. So, I will now summarize those events that led me to the conclusion that I was being watched over by someone.

If, in 1961, I had not agreed to take my friend to the recruiter, I would not have joined the Marine Corps.

If, on that day, we had not decided to go to the Fireman's Field Day, I would not have met my future wife.

If I had not extended my enlistment in 1963, we would not have been transferred to Hawaii.

If, in 1963 if the training accident occurred fifteen seconds sooner, I would most certainly have lost my life.

If, in 1963, I had not applied for NESEP, we would not have been transferred to Kansas.

If we had not been sent to Kansas, we would not have adopted our daughter.

If, in 1968, I had not left the NESEP program and I had been commissioned, I most certainly would have been sent to Vietnam as a Platoon Commander and very probably caused the death or injury to an unknown number of Marines due to my inability to control my temper.

If, in 1971, I had not applied for the SNCO Degree Completion Program, I would not have returned to Kansas to complete my degree.

If, in 1978, I had not requested a transfer to New River, we would not have bought Cougar for our daughter.

If, in 1981, I had chosen to take one of four opportunities I had to accept civilian employment, I would not have joined the Civil Service at the simulator building. One big reason for this was not wanting to move Cougar because all the options were hundreds of miles away.

If, in 1986, I had not survived my heart attack, this story would have ended.

If, in 1999, I had not moved to the MAO from the simulators, I would not have experienced the 7 Habits of Successful People which altered my temperament, not have moved to MCIEAST and reached the GS-13 level.

These events and occurrences are arguably not definite proof that they were the result of any supernatural intervention. At the same time, there is nothing to say that they were not. It reduces to a matter of faith. I choose to believe I was watched over and directed by the Lord, but that is my choice. The reader is, of course, free to make their own choice. I will cite a well-known statement; "HE moves in mysterious ways."

www.ingramcontent.com/pod-product-compliance
Lightning Source LLC
Chambersburg PA
CBHW051651120626
46551CB00015B/2307